Frank Mangelsdorf (Hg.)

EINST UND JETZT
UNIVERSITÄT POTSDAM

Text: Matthias Zimmermann
Übersetzung: Juliane Voigt

EDITION BRANDENBURG

Fotos: Karla Fritze: 13, 15, 17, 19, 21, 27, 29, 31, 35, 37, 39, 41, 63, 71, 73, 75, 77, 79, 81, 83, 87, 91, 93, 95; Dirk Laubner: 11, 45, 69; Thomas Roese: 25, 43, 47, 49, 51, 53, 55, 57, 59, 61, 65, 67, 85, 89; Matthias Zimmermann: 21, 33

Historische Aufnahmen: Karla Fritze: 10, 24, 44, 68, 76, 80, 84; Christoph Hauschildt: 72, 74; alle anderen: Fotoarchiv der Universität Potsdam

ISBN 978-3-941092-73-0

Die Deutsche Nationalbibliothek verzeichnet diese Publikation in der Deutschen Nationalbibliografie; detaillierte bibliografische Daten sind im Internet über http://dnb.d-nb.de abrufbar.

CULTURCON medien
Bernd Oeljeschläger

Choriner Straße 1, 10119 Berlin
Telefon 030/34398440, Telefax 030/34398442

Ottostraße 5, 27793 Wildeshausen
Telefon 04431/9559878, Telefax 04431/9559879

www.culturcon.de

Redaktion: Matthias Zimmermann, Karla Fritze (Universität Potsdam)
Gestaltung: Kathrin Strahl, Berlin
Druck: Silber Druck OHG, Niestetal
Berlin/Wildeshausen 2011

Für ihre Unterstützung danken wir:

Universität Potsdam

Universitätsgesellschaft Potsdam e. V.

Investitionsbank des Landes Brandenburg ILB

Studentenwerk Potsdam
Anstalt des öffentlichen Rechts

INHALT

Luftaufnahme Campus Am Neuen Palais, 1993.

Am westlichen Ende des Parks Sanssouci, direkt hinter dem Neuen Palais, liegt der Campus Am Neuen Palais. Seine Gebäude gehören zu den historischsten der Potsdamer Wissenschaftslandschaft: Ein Großteil des Campus stammt aus der Zeit Friedrichs des Großen. Nach dem Zweiten Weltkrieg fand hier auch der wissenschaftliche Neuanfang statt: Die hier beheimatete, 1948 gegründete Brandenburgische Landeshochschule, die von 1951 bis 1990 Pädagogische Hochschule hieß, war die größte in Brandenburg. Heute logieren die Hochschulverwaltung sowie die Institute der Philosophischen Fakultät und der Mathematik sowie die Sportwissenschaft am historischen Ort.

At the western end of Sanssouci Park, right behind the New Palace, the campus Am Neuen Palais can be found. Its buildings are amongst the most historic of Potsdam's scientific community: the majority of the campus' buildings originate from the time of Frederick the Great. After World War II scientific comeback also began here: the "Brandenburgische Landeshochschule", a state college founded in 1948, was the largest in Brandenburg. From 1951 to 1990 it was a teacher training college. Today the university's administration, the Faculty of Arts, and the institutes of sports sciences and mathematics are located at this historic site.

CAMPUS AM NEUEN PALAIS

Luftaufnahme Campus
Am Neuen Palais, 2010.

Blick vom Neuen Palais auf die Kolonnaden, 1960er Jahre.

Aus Alt wird Neu – und gewaltig: die Kolonnaden. Zwei Pavillons, von Obelisken bekrönt, 42 Skulpturen, insgesamt 122 Säulen und ein prachtvolles Mittelportal machen sie zum größten Natursteinbau im Park Sanssouci. Das Halbrund verbindet die beiden Communs, früher Gästehäuser und Wirtschaftsgebäude fürs Neue Palais, in denen die Universität Potsdam „residiert“, vor allem aber die Wiese im Zentrum des Campus mit der „Mopke“, einst Aufmarschplatz kaiserlicher Truppen, heute Schauplatz des musikalischen Höhepunkts der Potsdamer Schlössernacht.

What once was old is turned into something new – and enormous: the colonnades. Two pavilions, crowned by obelisks, 42 sculptures, 122 columns and a magnificent gate make it the largest construction made of natural stone in Sanssouci Park. The semicircle connects the two Communs, former guest and staff buildings of the New Palace, in which the university 'resides'. But it also connects the lawn in the centre of the campus with the "Mopke", a former parade square of the Emperor's troops, today setting for the musical highlights of "Potsdamer Schlössernacht" – an annual cultural event in Sanssouci Park.

In den Kolonnaden, 2008.

Blick zum Auditorium maximum der Pädagogischen Hochschule „Karl Liebknecht", 1970er Jahre.

Vom Neuen Palais kommend, geht man – heute wie früher – durch einen bezaubernden Kastanienhain auf jenes Gebäude zu, in dem das Auditorium maximum der Hochschule untergebracht ist. Einst stand vor dem Hauptportal eine Büste Karl Liebknechts, dessen Namen die Pädagogische Hochschule in Potsdam seit 1971 trug. Mit den großen Lettern am Haus verschwanden 1991, als die Universität Potsdam gegründet wurde, auch der Name und die Büste. Geblieben ist der Kastanienhain, der dem Vorplatz des Gebäudes, vor allem zur Blütezeit, den Charme eines Parks verleiht.

Coming from the New Palace one walks – today as back then – through a beautiful chestnut grove towards the building where the "auditorium maximum", the main lecture hall of the university is located. A bust portraying Karl Liebknecht, who had lent his name to the teacher training college since 1971, used to stand right in front of the main portal. When the University of Potsdam was founded in 1991, the name disappeared and with it went the large lettering and the bust. What remains is the chestnut grove, which grants the forecourt the charm of a park, especially when the trees are in bloom.

Blick zum Auditorium maximum der Universität Potsdam, 2011.

Kaiserlicher Marstall, 1894.

Das Auditorium maximum der Universität Potsdam kann sich sehen lassen, immerhin finden im festlichsten Saal der Hochschule gut 400 Menschen Platz. Doch auch die Geschichte dieses Raumes hat „Größe": Das Gebäude, in dem er sich befindet, diente einst als kaiserlicher Marstall. 1894 fertiggestellt, war die prachtvolle Reithalle vor allem Kaiser Wilhelm II. und seinen Pferden vorbehalten. Als der 1919 ins holländische Exil ging, folgten andere „Mieter": Post, Polizei, Militär. In den 1950er Jahren baute man eine Zwischendecke in die Halle ein und statt Pferd und Reiter zogen – quasi ins Dachgeschoss – Professoren und Studenten ein.

The auditorium maximum of the University of Potsdam is quite presentable; the festive hall seats about 400 people. But also the history of this room does not lack 'size': after all, the building in which the hall is located used to be the imperial stables. Finished in 1894 the magnificent indoor riding hall was reserved for Emperor William II and his horses. When he went into exile to the Netherlands in 1919, other 'tenants' moved in: the post, the police, the military. In the 1950s a suspended ceiling was built into the hall and instead of horses and riders professors and students moved into the attic, as it were.

Auditorium maximum der Universität Potsdam, 2011.

Südliches Commun-Gebäude, 1960er Jahre.

Es sind die beiden Communs, die der Universität Potsdam ihr Gesicht geben. Und das ist wörtlich gemeint: Das Logo der Hochschule zeigt die zum Neuen Palais gewandte Seite der Häuser mit den zwei halbrunden Treppen. Außerdem befindet sich im südlichen der beiden Gebäude die zentrale Hochschulleitung. Dabei war der Bau ursprünglich alles andere als „herrschaftlich“: In der Zeit nach seiner Erbauung 1766 – 1769 beherbergte es die Küche und „Kammern für die Dienerschaft“, bestenfalls Räume für königliche Kavaliere. Mittlerweile steht das namensgebende „commun“ weniger für „gemein“ als für gemeinsam, da im Haus zugleich viele Lehrveranstaltungen stattfinden. Und die Wiese davor ist ohnehin für alle da.

It's the "Communs" (French, 'common') that give the university its face – literally. The university's logo shows the side of the buildings with its two semicircular stairs that are facing the New Palace. The president's office and the central administration offices of the university are located in the southern building. However, the buildings were initially anything but 'stately': after their erection from 1766 to 1769 the kitchen and the chambers for the domestic staff were located here, rooms of the royal cavalry at best. Nowadays "Commun" stands less for 'common' than for 'jointly' because many lectures and courses are being held in the building as well. And the lawn can be used by everybody, anyway.

Südliches Commun-Gebäude, 2011.

Nördliches Commun-Gebäude und der symmetrische Nachbau des Marstalls, 1960er Jahre.

Der Geist vergangener Zeiten durchweht auch das nördliche der beiden Communs-Gebäude: Ursprünglich war es ein Gästehaus für Besucher des Königs, wenn auch ein spartanisches: „Zwei eiserne Bettstellen, zwei ordinaire Matratzen, (...) ein Nachtstuhl, (...) zwei Schemel", mehr gab es nicht für des Königs Gäste um 1799. Das änderte sich gewiss nicht, als das Gebäude im 19. Jahrhundert zur (wohl ansehnlichsten) preußischen Kaserne wurde und die I. Kompanie des Kgl. Lehr- und Infanteriebataillons aufnahm. Erst nach dem Zweiten Weltkrieg zog mit der Pädagogischen Hochschule ein neuer Geist in die Räume des Hauses. Inzwischen bildet es den Sitz der Philosophischen Fakultät.

The ghost of past times also wafts through the northern of the two Communs: it used to be a guesthouse for the king's visitors. But it was equipped quite spartanly: "two iron bedsteads, two ordinary mattresses, (...) one commode, (...) two stools" and nothing more for the king's guests around 1799. That definitely did not change when the building was turned into barracks – the most presentable Prussian barracks as it were – and the 1st company of the royal demonstration and infantry battalion moved in. Only after World War II, when the teacher training college moved into the premises, did a different spirit move in as well. Today it houses the Faculty of Arts.

Nördliches Commun-Gebäude und Haus der Sportwissenschaft und -medizin, 2011.

Blick in den Innenhof des ehemaligen Kutschenhofes, 1985.

Neben den größeren Communs-Gebäuden gab es kleinere Ställe und Remisen für königliche Kutschen. Nach dem Zweiten Weltkrieg wurden sie als Garagen und Laborräume genutzt. Erst durch den Neubau der Bibliothek für den Campus Am Neuen Palais erhielt der frühere Kutschenhof ein völlig anderes Aussehen. Eine Konstruktion aus Glas und Beton „schwebt" gleichsam im Hof und präsentiert sich als Verbindung von modernster Bibliotheksausstattung und historischem Ambiente. 120 000 Bände des Bestands der Philosophischen Fakultät stehen hier; dazu kommen 170 Arbeitsplätze – mit königlichem Ausblick.

Next to the Communs there are smaller buildings which were used as stables and depots for the royal carriages. After World War II these buildings were used as garages and laboratories. Only when the new library for the campus Am Neuen Palais was built, did the former carriages yard get a completely new look. A construction of glass and concrete seems to 'float' inside the yard and presents itself as a combination of modern library facilities and historic ambience. 120,000 volumes of the Faculty of Arts' stock are stored here; additionally there are 170 seats – with a royal view.

BIBLIOTHEK IM KUTSCHENHOF

Bibliotheksneubau auf dem Campus Am Neuen Palais, 2011.

Sporthalle im Nachbau des Marstalls, 1970er Jahre.

Während es im Marstall, dem heutigen Audimax, schon zu Zeiten von Kaiser Wilhelm II. sportlich zuging, ist die Sporthalle im Haus 12, dem Sitz der Sportwissenschaft, eine Nachkriegsschöpfung. Obwohl äußerlich kaum vom königlichen Pferdedomizil zu unterscheiden, wurde das symmetrisch dazu angelegte Gebäude erst in den 1950er Jahren erbaut. Dort gab es von Beginn an ein Schwimmbecken im Keller und eine Sporthalle im Obergeschoss. Die Sportwissenschaft der Universität ist längst über die Mauern des Gebäudes hinaus gewachsen. Doch die Sporthalle mit Ausblick auf den Park besteht noch immer.

While the former royal stables, today's Audimax, have been used for sportive purposes since the times of Emperor William II, the gymnasium in house 12, which houses the institute of sports sciences, is a postwar creation. Although it is hardly distinguishable from the royal stables the symmetrically constructed premises was only built in the 1950s. From the beginning there was a swimming pool in the basement and a gymnasium on the top floor. The institute of sports sciences has long ago grown beyond the walls of the building. But the gymnasium with a view on the park has remained.

Sporthalle des Campus Am Neuen Palais, 2011.

Schwimmbecken im Keller der Marstallkopie, 1960er Jahre.

Als von 1954 bis 1958 das heutige Haus 12 errichtet wurde, erhielten die dort untergebrachten Sportstudenten im Keller sogar ein eigenes Schwimmbecken für ihr Training. In den ersten Jahren nach der Gründung der Universität wurde es noch genutzt. Heute besteht es nicht mehr. In den südöstlichen Flügel des Gebäudes ist 2007 die Hochschulambulanz eingezogen, die sich vor allem um die Sportler kümmert. Als Medizinisches Untersuchungszentrum des Deutschen Olympischen Sportbundes werden hier aber nicht nur Untersuchungen, Physiotherapie und Leistungsbestimmungen durchgeführt, sondern auch Lehre und Forschung betrieben.

When house 12 was built between 1954 and 1958 the sport students got their own swimming pool for training purposes in the basement. In the first years after the founding of the university it was still used, but not anymore. The university's outpatient clinic moved into the south-eastern wing of the building, where athletes are treated in particular. As a medical examination centre of the German Olympic Sports Confederation they perform examinations, physical therapy and performance diagnostics but also teach and do research.

Therapieraum der Hochschulambulanz, 2011.

Obere Mensa der Pädagogischen Hochschule, 1966.

Nein, Filzpantoffeln wie im Neuen Palais braucht man für die Obere Mensa auf dem Campus Am Neuen Palais nicht, aber den Vergleich mit den Sälen des königlichen Palastes braucht der bis 2011 sanierte Raum auch nicht zu scheuen. Stäbchenparkett, rote Pilaster und modernste Technik zeichnen ihn als etwas Besonderes aus. Auch die beiden anderen vom Studentenwerk betreuten Mensen in Golm und Griebnitzsee sind gänzlich neu gestaltet worden. Doch eine Komplettausstattung als Veranstaltungssaal mit Bühne, Flügel und Veranstaltungstechnik gibt es vorerst nur am Neuen Palais. Vielleicht macht man ja bald dem benachbarten Schlosstheater Konkurrenz?

No, you will not need felt slippers for the upper cafeteria on the campus Am Neuen Palais, as they use them in the New Palace. But the newly renovated room, which was re-opened in April 2011, does not have to shy away from the comparison with the halls of the royal palace. Wooden flooring, red pilaster and the most modern technical equipment distinguish it amongst the three cafeterias of the student services office, although the other cafeterias in Golm and Griebnitzsee have been entirely remodeled as well. But a cafeteria fully equipped as an event location with stage, piano and event technology so far only exists at Am Neuen Palais. Maybe soon the upper cafeteria will compete with the palace theater?

Obere Mensa, 2011.

Studentenfest auf den Treppen der Communs, 1979.

Geschichte braucht stets Kulissen, vor denen sie sich präsentiert. In Potsdam gibt es davon viele. Eine, wenn auch nicht die prominenteste, bilden die Freitreppen der beiden Communs. Sie schwingen sich als Halbrund auf die „Mopke" hinunter, jenen Vorplatz des Neuen Palais, der seinen Namen der eigentümlichen holländischen Pflasterung verdankt. Friedrich II. setzte mit ihnen seinem Triumph im Siebenjährigen Krieg ein Denkmal, Kaiser Wilhelm II. erschien hier jährlich volksnah zum Schrippenfest. Margot Honecker beschritt die Treppen zur Hochschulbegehung und auch Bundespräsident Roman Herzog kam sie schon herauf. Geschichte ist am Neuen Palais in nahezu jedem Stein. Erst durch die Studenten aber, die sich die Treppen zu Eigen gemacht haben, bekommen sie einen besonderen Charme und das Äußere der Universität ein Gesicht.

History always needs a setting in front of which it can present itself. There are a lot of those in Potsdam. One of them, if not the most prominent one, are the outside staircases of the two "Communs", which come down in a semicircle towards the "Mopke", the front yard of the New Palace, which got its name from the typical Dutch pavement. Frederick II showcased his triumph in the Seven Year's War with these staircases. Emperor William II celebrated here the "Schrippenfest" (a festival of the demonstration battalion every year on Pentecost) among the common people. Margot Honecker climbed these stairs on the occasion of a tour of the former teacher training college and even the former Federal President Roman Herzog came up these stairs. One can find history in almost every stone at campus Am Neuen Palais. But only because of the students, who adopted the staircase as their own, did they get a specific charm and gave the university outside a face.

Studenten auf den Treppen der Communs, 2011.

Gewächshaus und Sitz der Botanik der Pädagogischen Hochschule, 1960er Jahre.

Als Friedrich II. den Park Sanssouci anlegen ließ, war schnell klar: Hier braucht es einen Gärtner, und zwar direkt vor Ort. So war das dem Park angeschlossene Areal an der Maulbeerallee schon seit dem 18. Jahrhundert Sitz der Hofgärtnerei. Ab 1840 legte der Hofgärtner Hermann Sello dann nach Plänen von Peter Joseph Lenné den malerischen „Paradiesgarten" an. Das berühmte Haus des Hofgärtners, das Ludwig Persius im italienischen Stil entworfen hatte, steht nicht mehr. 1910 wurde es abgerissen und weiter westlich bei den Gewächshäusern ein Neubau errichtet. Die „Villa Kache" und die anderen Gebäude des Botanischen Gartens beherbergen heute Teile des Instituts für Biochemie und Biologie.

When Frederick II had built Sanssouci Park it soon became evident that a gardener was needed right on the grounds. Thus the site close to the park, at Maulbeerallee, has been the domicile of the court gardener since the 18th century. In 1840 the court gardener Hermann Sello designed the picturesque "Paradise Garden" according to the plans of Peter Joseph Lenné. The famous house of the court gardener which was designed by Ludwig Persius in an Italian style does not exist anymore. It was torn down in 1910 and a new house was build further west near the greenhouses. Today the "Villa Kache" and the other buildings of the botanical garden are the domicile of parts of the institute for biochemistry and biology.

Gewächshaus und Sitz der Botanik der Universität Potsdam, 2011.

Gewächshaus, 1960er Jahre.

Im „Paradiesgarten“ des Botanischen Gartens finden sich auf ca. 2,5 Hektar Tausende einzigartige Pflanzen: Ein Steppen- und Heidegarten, eine Frühblüher- und eine Wildblumenwiese, ein Teich mit Sumpf- und Wasserpflanzen sowie ein Alpinum mit Gebirgspflanzen aus Europa, Asien und Nordamerika ermöglichen dem Besucher eine botanische Weltreise. Kleinod des Gartens sind die öffentlich zugänglichen Gewächshäuser, in denen auf circa 3 000 Quadratmetern rund 4 600 tropische und subtropische Pflanzenarten kultiviert werden. Palmen, Kakteen, Orchideen, Farne, aber auch zahlreiche Nutz- und Kulturpflanzen wachsen hier.

In the "Paradise Garden" on the premises of the botanical garden thousands of unique plants spread over 2.5 hectares: a steppe and moorland garden, a spring and wild flowers field, a pond with swamp and water plants or an alpine area with mountain flora from Europe, Asia and North America allow the visitor a botanical trip around the world. The garden's gems are the greenhouses in which about 4,600 tropical and subtropical plants are cultivated on about 3,000 square metres and which are open to the public. Palms, cacti, orchids, ferns but also cultivated plants and agricultural crops are grown here.

Kakteenhaus, 2009.

Eröffnung des Studentenkellers der Pädagogischen Hochschule „Karl Liebknecht“, 1972.

Studentische Kultur findet auf dem Campus Am Neuen Palais überwiegend im Untergrund statt, und das ganz freiwillig. In den Gewölben des Nord-Commun logiert der „Nil“-Studentenkeller. Schon 1972 eroberten die Studenten der Pädagogischen Hochschule „Karl Liebknecht“ die historischen Gemäuer für sich und richteten die Räume als Studentenclub ein. Der „Nil“ macht nun seit 1998 Kultur für Studierende. Und ist damit in Potsdam nicht allein: Schon seit 1994 gibt es die Studentenkneipe „Pub à la Pub“ in der Innenstadt, und das seit 2005 bestehende studentische Kulturzentrum „Kuze“ in den Elflein-Höfen ist längst zur Heimat zahlreicher Initiativen geworden.

Student culture at the campus Am Neuen Palais is mostly underground – voluntarily. The vaults of the northern Commun house the student's club "Nil". Already in 1972 did the students of the teacher training college take over the historic rooms and made them into a student club. The "Nil" has been presenting cultural programmes for students since 1998. And it's not the only one in Potsdam: since 1994 the student pub "Pub à la Pub" can be found in the city centre and the student's cultural centre "Kuze" in the courts at Hermann-Elflein-Straße has been home to different initiatives since 2005.

„Nil“-Studentenkeller, 2011.

Auf dem Gelände der Pädagogischen Hochschule, 1960er Jahre.

Hörsaal, Mensa, Lesesaal – der studentische Kosmos wäre nicht vollständig, würde er nicht durch Orte ergänzt, die mit der Zeit ganz selbstverständlich durch die Studierenden in Besitz genommen werden. Am Neuen Palais sind das die zahlreichen Wiesen. Freilich ist das auch zu Zeiten der Pädagogischen Hochschule schon so gewesen. Allein die „politisch-hintersinnige" Beschallungsanlage zur ideologischen Lernunterstützung verrät das Bild aus einer anderen Wirklichkeit. Keine Angst: Es gibt sie längst nicht mehr – die Wiese aber schon.

Lecture hall, cafeteria, reading hall – the students cosmos would not be the same had it not been complemented by places which were quite naturally taken over by the students over the years. At the campus Am Neuen Palais it's mostly the lawns. As a matter of fact it's been that way since the times of the former teacher training college. Only the 'politically subtle' loudspeaker system for ideological learning support is evidence of a different reality. But not to worry: this system is long gone, only the lawn remains.

Campuswiese, 2011.

Pferdestall des kaiserlichen Marstalls, 1894.

Für einen Kaffee, ein Stück Kuchen oder ein Eis gehen viele auf dem Campus Am Neuen Palais gern in die Cafeteria. Die wenigsten von ihnen wissen, dass dort, wo sie sich an einen der Tische setzen, vor gut 100 Jahren die Pferde Kaiser Wilhelms II. standen. In den Seitenflügeln des damaligen Marstalls befanden sich u.a. vier Ställe für insgesamt 85 Pferde. Dank der behutsamen Restaurierung des Raumes bei seiner Umgestaltung zur Cafeteria kann man den Aufbau der früheren Stallanlagen heute noch erahnen. Hafer und Stroh stehen zum Glück nicht mehr auf der Speisekarte.

Many people like to go to the cafeteria at campus Am Neuen Palais for a cup of coffee, a piece of cake or ice cream. Only few know that where they are sitting there used to be the horses of Emperor William II about 100 years ago. The side wings of the former royal stables housed four stables for 85 horses altogether. Thanks to the cautious restoration when the room was turned into a cafeteria one might still get an idea of the former layout. Luckily hay and straw are no longer on the menu.

Cafeteria, 2011.

Sportfest der Pädagogischen Hochschule, 1960er Jahre.

Leibesübungen oder Pausenexpress, Bestenermittlung oder Hochschulsport – körperliche Bewegung hat Tradition an Potsdamer Hochschulen. Trat man bei den Sportfesten der Pädagogischen Hochschule noch in Kittel und Pullunder gegeneinander an, hat sich der Hochschulsport seit der Gründung der Universität 1991 enorm entwickelt. Rund 400 Sportkurse für insgesamt 7 000 aktive Sportler werden derzeit pro Semester angeboten, Disziplingrenzen gibt es nicht. Dazu kommen zwei Fitnesscenter. 2010 wurde der Potsdamer Hochschulsport als Deutschlands bester ausgezeichnet. Höhepunkt des Jahres ist nach wie vor das Sportfest im Sommer. Wer dazu im Laborkittel kommt, darf trotzdem mitmachen.

Exercise, competitions and sports – physical training has a long tradition at Potsdam's colleges and universities. While students lined up in lab coats and slipovers at sport events in times of the former teacher training college, sports have come a long way since the foundation of the University of Potsdam in 1991. About 400 sports classes for 7,000 active sports men and women are offered every semester, and there is no limit to the sport disciplines. Two fitness centres can be added to the list. In 2010 the university's sports programme was decorated as the best in Germany. Highlight of the year is still the sports festival in the summer. And whoever turns up in a lab coat may compete nonetheless.

Hochschulsportfest, 2010.

Luftaufnahme Campus Golm, 1993.

Am Stadtrand von Potsdam, in Golm, befindet sich der größte der drei Standorte der Universität Potsdam. In den 1930er Jahren als Kasernengelände angelegt, wurde es bis 1945 vom Nachrichtendienst der Luftwaffe genutzt. 1951 entstand hier die sogenannte „Juristische Hochschule Potsdam-Eiche“ des Ministeriums für Staatssicherheit, an der bis 1990 Juristen für den Dienst beim MfS ausgebildet wurden. Seit der Gründung der Universität sind die Humanwissenschaftliche und die Mathematisch-Naturwissenschaftliche Fakultät überwiegend hier beheimatet. Gemeinsam mit den Instituten des Wissenschaftsparks Golm bilden sie Brandenburgs größtes Forschungsareal.

The largest of the three campuses is located at the outskirts of Potsdam, in Golm. In the 1930s barracks were established on the site and used by the air force intelligence until 1945. From 1951 the Ministry for State Security used the premises for the so-called "Juristische Hochschule Potsdam-Eiche", a law school. Jurists were educated here for their service in the Ministry for State Security until 1990. Since the foundation of the university it houses mainly the Faculty of Human Sciences and the Faculty of Mathematics and Natural Sciences. Together with the institutes of the Potsdam-Golm Science Park it is Brandenburg's largest research site.

Luftaufnahme Campus Golm, 2010.

Eingangsbereich zum Campus Golm, 1993.

Mit ihren derzeit rund 20 000 Studierenden gehört die Universität Potsdam zu den mittelgroßen Hochschulen in Deutschland. 1991 gegründet, ist sie mit ihren fünf Fakultäten an drei Standorten stetig gewachsen. Nahezu alle vorhandenen Gebäude der Universität wurden seit ihrer Gründung saniert und modernisiert, viele neue entstanden: Labors, Hörsäle und Seminarräume, Büros und Bibliotheken. Zahlreiche Vorhaben können auch dank der Einwerbung von Drittmitteln verwirklicht werden, bei anderen hilft oft die Universitätsgesellschaft. 20 Jahre nach ihrer Gründung befindet sich die Universität im Aufbruch. Schon wieder, immer noch.

With about 20,000 students the University of Potsdam is one of the medium-sized universities in Germany. Founded in 1991, with five faculties spread out over three campuses it has grown ever since. Almost every building of the university has been renovated or remodeled since the foundation and many new ones have been built: laboratories, lecture halls and class rooms, offices and libraries. Numerous building projects can be realized because of the raising of third-party funds. Others are financed with the help of the university society. 20 years after its foundation the university is on the go.

Studenten am Eingang zum Campus Golm, 2011.

Hauptgebäude der „Juristischen Hochschule Potsdam-Eiche", 1989.

Einst zur sogenannten „Juristischen Hochschule Potsdam-Eiche" gehörend, wird in dem markanten Neubau im Eingangsbereich des Golmer Campus inzwischen ganz anderen Fragen nachgegangen. Der Hauptsitz der Humanwissenschaftlichen Fakultät nimmt v.a. die Bildungswissenschaften und den Exzellenzbereich Kognitionswissenschaften auf, die sich hier nach und nach ihre Labors einrichten. Wie das BabyLab, in dem die Kleinsten als Entdecker und Entdeckte im Zentrum stehen. Ihre Fähigkeiten, ihre Sprache und ihr Denken werden hier in zahlreichen Forschungsprojekten untersucht. Und das ist erst der Anfang, nicht nur für die Babys.

The most prominent building at the entrance of Golm campus used to be part of the former law school. Today a very different discourse is taking place here. It is the main building of the Faculty of Human Sciences and houses first and foremost the Department of Educational Studies and the Area of Excellence: Cognitive Sciences, their offices and laboratories. One of those is the BabyLab, where the youngest are at the centre of research. Their abilities, their language and their ways of thinking are explored in various research projects. And that is only the beginning, not only for the babies.

Haupthaus der Humanwissenschaftlichen Fakultät im Ausbau, 2011.

Studentenwohnheim und Gebäude der Musikwissenschaft, Anfang 1990er Jahre.

In Golm ist Musik drin. Seit der Gründung der Universität Potsdam wurden die z.T. in den 1930er Jahren entstandenen Gebäude des Ensembles vollständig saniert. In den historischen Häusern befinden sich heute vor allem die Departments der Humanwissenschaftlichen Fakultät, darunter die Lehrerbildung und die Musikwissenschaft, die sogar über einen eigenen Kammermusiksaal verfügt. Daneben sind auch Teile des Instituts für Erd- und Umweltwissenschaften hier untergebracht. Das Militär gibt hier schon lange nicht mehr den Ton an. Stattdessen ist Golm der Welt ein Stückchen näher gekommen.

Apart from science there is also music in Golm. Since the foundation of the University of Potsdam most of the buildings on the campus have been renovated completely, because some of them have been existing since the 1930s. In those historic buildings, which had been planned as military barracks, reside the departments of the Human Sciences including the department of teacher training and musicology. The musicology even has a chamber music hall available. Furthermore parts of the institute of earth and environmental sciences are housed in these bulidings. The military does no longer dominate here. Instead Golm has come closer to the big, wide world.

Studentenwohnheim und Gebäude der Musikwissenschaft, 2011.

Baufläche für die Naturwissenschaften in Golm, 1997.

Als nach der Gründung der Universität Potsdam beschlossen wurde, die Mathematisch-Naturwissenschaftliche Fakultät langfristig in Golm anzusiedeln, gab es dort neben den historischen Gebäuden nur eines: eine grüne Wiese. Also entstand ein heute zentraler Teil des Campus völlig neu. Vier große Gebäude wurden in den vergangenen Jahren für die einzelnen Institute gebaut und mit modernsten Labors, Hörsälen und Büros ausgestattet. Und schon jetzt sind weitere Häuser geplant. Die Wiese fängt in Golm zum Glück noch immer hinter dem letzten Haus an.

After the foundation of the university it was decided that the Faculty of Mathematics and Natural Sciences should take up a long-term residence in Golm. Apart from the historic buildings only one thing existed in Golm back then: a green field. So today's central part of the campus arose completely new. Four huge buildings have been built in the last years for the several institutes, equipped with modern laboratories, lecture halls and offices. And other buildings are planned. Fortunately, the green field in Golm still begins behind the last building.

Haus der Chemie auf dem Campus Golm, 2011.

Bibliothek der „Juristischen Hochschule Potsdam-Eiche", 1989.

Wie die Wissenschaft selbst, wachsen auch die in ihr gewonnenen Erkenntnisse rasant an: Neue Bibliotheken an allen drei Standorten der Universität Potsdam zeigen das gewandelte Gesicht unserer Wissensgesellschaft, zuletzt das 2011 fertiggestellte Informations-, Kommunikations- und Medienzentrum (IKMZ) in Golm. Wer im „Schwarzen Diamanten" ein Buch sucht, sollte besser wissen, wo. Platz für insgesamt eine Million Bände hat das neue „Haupthaus" der Universitätsbibliothek, in dem auch der Universitätsverlag zu Hause ist. Auf rund 6 800 Quadratmetern gibt es außerdem 476 Arbeits- und 80 PC-Arbeitsplätze.

Just like science itself the findings obtained by it grow and develop just as fast: new libraries at all three campuses of the University of Potsdam indicate the changed face of our knowledge society; recently the completion of the Information, Communication and Media Center in Golm in 2011. Whoever is searching for a book in the rooms of the 'Black Diamond' should better know where to look. The new 'principal building' of the university's library can hold up to one million books. Furthermore, it offers 476 work stations and 80 PC-equipped work stations on 6,800 square metres.

Informations- und Kommunikationszentrums in Golm, 2011.

Einweihung der Zuganbindung nach Golm, 1995.

Drei Standorte, auf das ganze Stadtgebiet verteilt, haben die Potsdamer Universität zu einem „abwechslungsreichen Reiseziel“ gemacht und ihre Verknüpfung zu einem logistischen Kraftakt. Busse, Straßen- und S-Bahnen sowie der Regionalverkehr der Deutschen Bahn verbinden sie miteinander. Und mit Berlin. Immerhin lebt ein Großteil der Potsdamer Studenten in der Hauptstadt und reist bequem mit dem Zug an. Das war nicht immer so. Früher glich eine Fahrt vom Bahnhof Zoo einer Weltreise. Inzwischen kommt alle 30 Minuten ein Zug aus Berlin am Neuen Palais oder in Golm an, in Griebnitzsee bringen die S-Bahnen im 10-Minuten-Takt Studenten und Mitarbeiter heran. Meistens sogar pünktlich.

Three campuses, spread over the whole city of Potsdam, make the university a varied destination and its connection a logistic tour de force. Busses, trams, the S-Bahn as well as the regional trains of Deutsche Bahn, Germany's national railway company, connect the campuses with one another. But they also connect the campuses to Berlin because the majority of the students lives in the capital and uses public transportation every day. But it was not always like this. A trip from the station Berlin Zoologischer Garten was like a trip around the world. Today every 30 minutes a train from Berlin arrives at campus Am Neuen Palais or Golm. In Griebnitzsee students and employees arrive by S-Bahn every ten minutes. Usually they are even on time.

Ankommende Studenten auf dem neuen Bahnhof in Golm, 2011.

Bau der Max-Planck-Institute, 1996.

In Golm ist in futuristischen Stahl-, Glas- und Betonkonstruktionen Natur zu Hause. Besser gesagt: die Erforschung der Natur. Der Wissenschaftspark Golm vereint auf einer Gesamtfläche von über 50 Hektar internationale Spitzenforschung von der Biotechnologie bis zur Gravitationsphysik, von der auch die Studierenden der Universität Potsdam enorm profitieren. Mit drei Max-Planck-Instituten, die Grundlagenforschung betreiben, und zwei Instituten der Fraunhofer-Gesellschaft mit dem Fokus auf anwendungsorientierter Forschung ist der Wissenschaftspark der größte naturwissenschaftliche Standort des Landes und wichtigster Partner der Mathematisch-Naturwissenschaftlichen Fakultät.

In Golm nature is at home in futuristic steel, glass and concrete constructions. Or rather the research of nature is at home here. The science park Golm unites international cutting-edge research from biotechnology to gravitational physics on an area of more than 50 hectares. The students of the university also benefit from that. With three Max Planck Institutes, which perform fundamental research, and two institutes of the Fraunhofer-Gesellschaft, which focus on application-oriented research, the science park is the largest scientific site in Brandenburg and the most important partner of the Faculty of Mathematics and Natural Sciences.

Max-Planck-Institute im Wissenschaftspark Golm, 2011.

Studentinnen beim Physikpraktikum, 1974.

Klappern gehört zum Handwerk – und ein Praktikum zu jedem Studium. Mehr denn je ist heute die Ausbildung an der Universität mit praktischen Erfahrungen verbunden. Jeder, der studiert, macht sich frühzeitig auf in „sein Feld", wobei das manchmal sogar wörtlich zu nehmen ist. Ob als Geologin auf Exkursion, Lehramtsstudent im Klassenzimmer, angehender Psychologe in der Beratungsstelle oder Chemiediplomandin im Labor. Wissenschaft will eben – auch in Potsdam – immer schneller vom Kopf in die Hände.

Puff is part of the trade, and a practical is part of one's studies. Today the education at the university is combined with practical experience more than ever. Everybody who studies has to 'to go into his or her field' at an early stage, which applies to many literally: as a geologist on a field trip, teacher trainee in a class room, prospective psychologist at the psychological counseling service or chemistry graduand in a lab. Students want to get hands on experience as soon as possible – in Potsdam as well as anywhere.

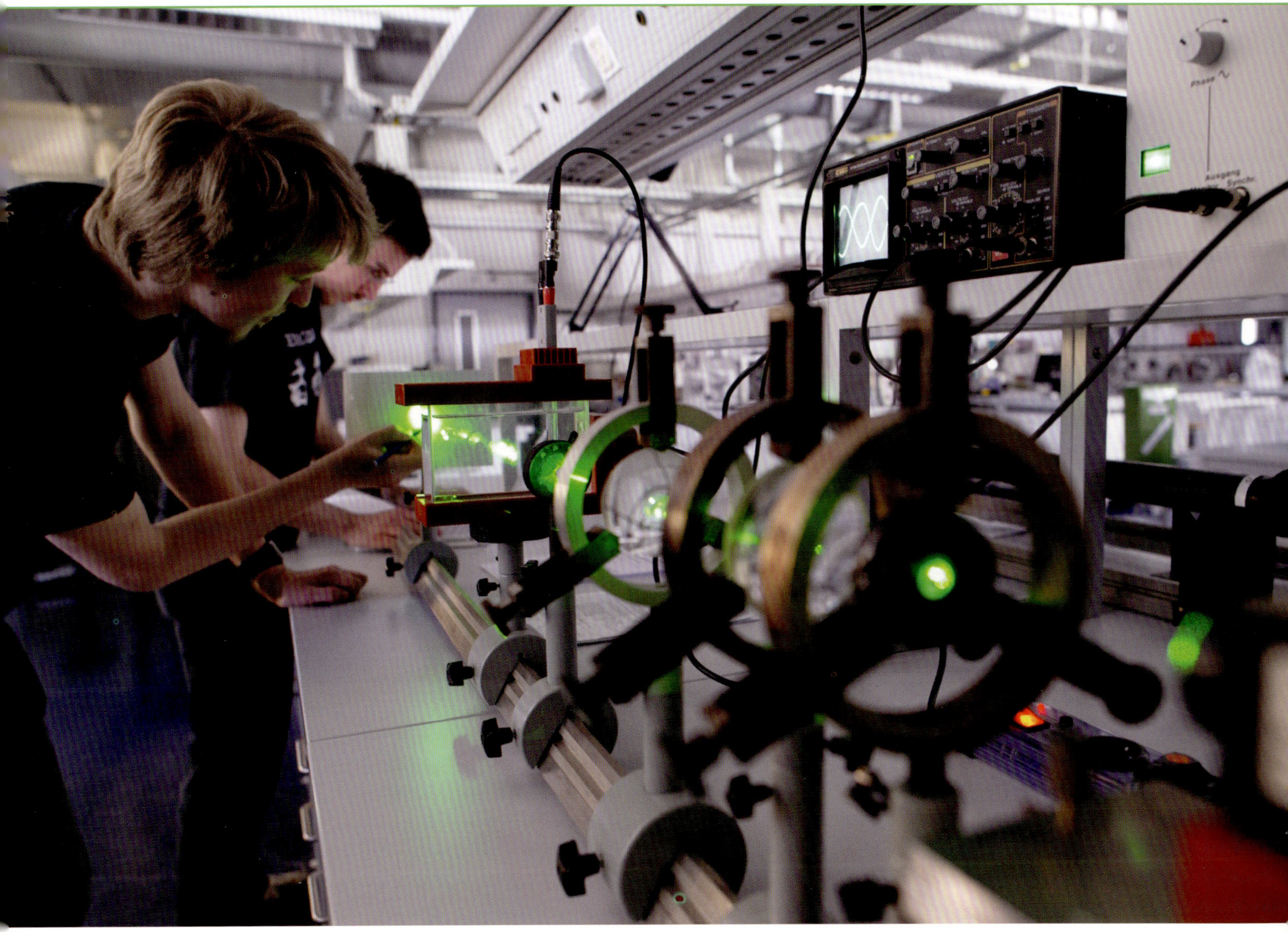

Studenten beim Physikpraktikum, 2011.

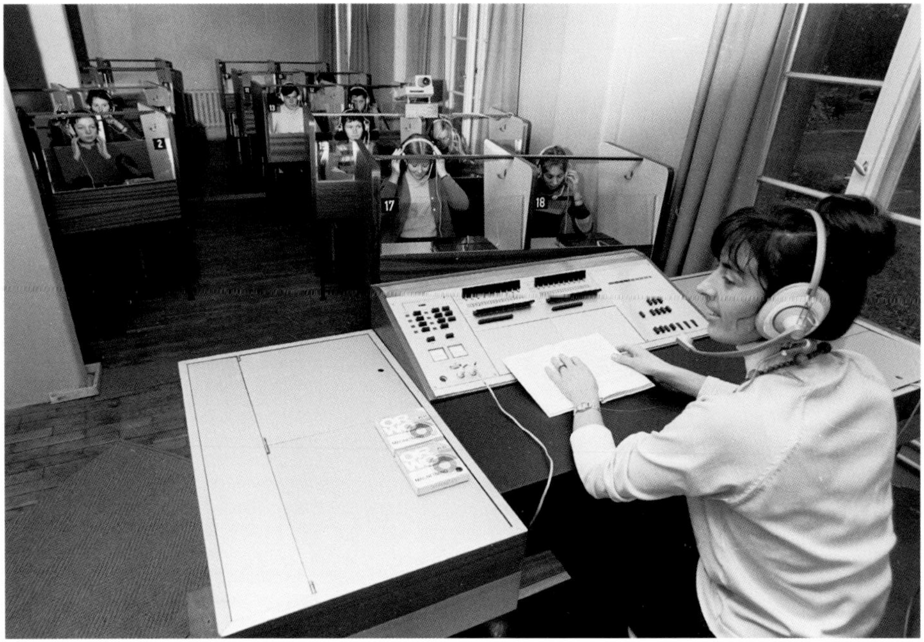

Fremdsprachenkabinett für Frontalunterricht, 1974.

Wer sprechen will, muss hören. So oder ähnlich könnte eine der Grundregeln beim Lernen einer fremden Sprache lauten. Durch die Lehrerbildung, die es in Potsdam seit der Zeit der Pädagogischen Hochschule gibt, wird an den drei Standorten der Universität Potsdam schon länger vielsprachig gehört, gesprochen und gelernt: Englisch, Französisch, Italienisch, Polnisch, Russisch, Spanisch und natürlich Deutsch – nicht zu vergessen all jene Muttersprachen, mit denen Studierende und Wissenschaftler schon aus ihrer Heimat hierher kommen. Für sie alle sind die neu eingerichteten Sprachlabors unverzichtbare Hilfe und Ort für Entdeckungen.

Whoever wants to speak has to listen. The basic rule for learning a new language could be something like that. Due to the classes for future pedagogical staff, which exist since the time of the teacher training college, a lot of people listen, speak and learn at all three campuses. One can hear and learn English, French, Italian, Polish, Russian, Spanish and of course German – not to mention all the different native languages the various students and scientists bring with them from their home countries. For all of them the newly equipped language laboratories are an indispensable help and place of discoveries.

Multimedia-Fachlabor für den direkten Austausch der Lernenden, 2008.

Labor der Organischen Chemie, um 1968.

Exzellente Forschung ist in Zeiten des stärker werdenden Wettbewerbs zwischen Universitäten um staatliche Gelder immer öfter von erfolgreicher Drittmitteleinwerbung abhängig. Wie richtungweisend sie für eine Universität sein können, zeigt der Blick auf den Haushalt der Universität Potsdam. Allein 2009 wurden 43 Millionen Euro an Drittmitteln eingeworben – immerhin acht Millionen mehr als im Jahr zuvor. Bereits jeder dritte Euro, der von der Hochschule ausgegeben wird, wurde von den Wissenschaftlern selbst eingeworben. 2011 wurden über 700 Stellen mithilfe dieser Gelder finanziert.

In times of competition among universities for state funds excellent research is more and more often dependent on successful acquisition of third-party funds. One look at the budget of the University of Potsdam shows just how trend-setting this can be. In 2009 alone, 43 million Euros have been raised – eight million more than in the year before. Almost every third Euro that is spent by the university was raised by the scientists themselves. In 2011 over 700 jobs have been financed with these funds.

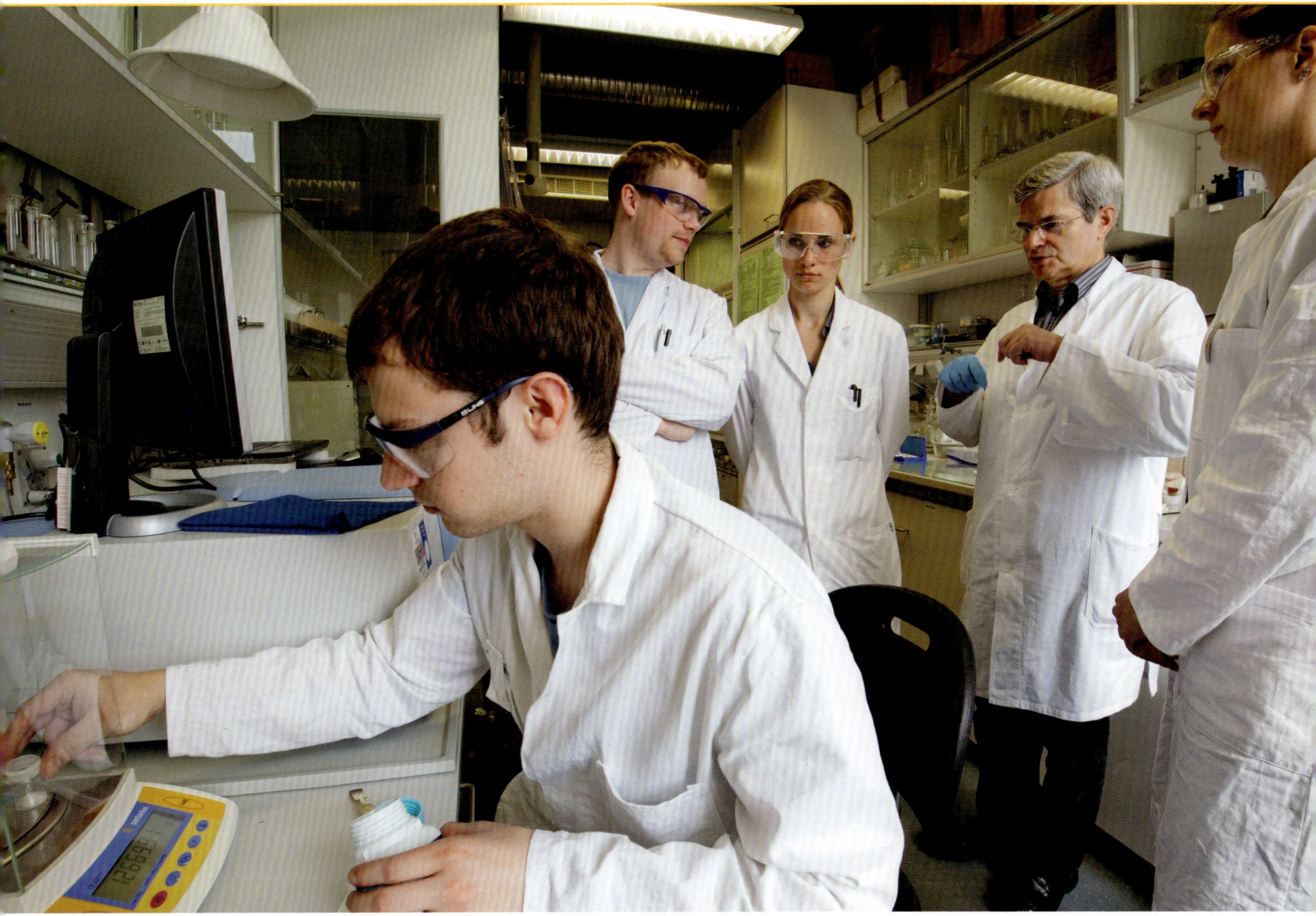

Labor der Anorganischen Chemie, 2011.

Labor der Organischen Chemie, um 1968.

Kolben, Bunsenbrenner und Schutzbrille findet man in einem Labor – wie in den 1960er Jahren – heute noch. Ansonsten hat sich seitdem so ziemlich alles verändert im Forschungsalltag der Naturwissenschaftler. Neue Ausstattung und Techniken prägen aber mittlerweile nicht nur deren Arbeit. Auch Psychologen, Sportwissenschaftler und selbst Geisteswissenschaftler sind dank neuer Untersuchungs- und Wissenstechnologien längst technisiert. Mit dieser Entwicklung Schritt zu halten, ist eine der Herausforderungen des 21. Jahrhunderts – auch für die Universität Potsdam.

Flasks, Bunsen burners and protective goggles could also be found in a lab of the 1960s. Other than that a lot has changed in the everyday research work of the natural scientists since these days. But new technical equipment and techniques do not only define the work of these scientists but also psychologists, sports scientists and even humanist scholars are engineered due to new research and scientific technologies. Keeping up with these new developments is one of the challenges of the 21st century, also for the University of Potsdam.

Labor der Anorganischen Chemie, 2011.

Luftaufnahme Campus Griebnitzsee, 1993.

Der Campus Griebnitzsee ist Sitz der Juristischen und der Wirtschafts- und Sozialwissenschaftlichen Fakultät. Von 1952 bis 1991 befand sich hier die Akademie für Staats- und Rechtswissenschaft der DDR. Nach ihrer Auflösung übernahm die Universität Potsdam das Gelände. Inzwischen ist der Campus enorm gewachsen, sind zu den vorhandenen Häusern zahlreiche Neubauten hinzugekommen. Neben einem großen Gebäude für die beiden ansässigen Fakultäten ist auch die Informatik in ein neu errichtetes Haus gezogen.

The Griebnitzsee campus is home to the Faculty of Economics and Social Sciences and the Law Faculty. The academy of political science and jurisprudence of the GDR resided on this site from 1952 to 1991. When the academy was closed the University of Potsdam took over the premises. Since then the campus has grown enormously and several buildings have been added to the already existing ones. Apart from a huge building for the two faculties, the institute of computer sciences also moved into a new building.

Luftaufnahme Campus Griebnitzsee, 2010.

Hauptgebäude der Akademie für Staats- und Rechtswissenschaft der DDR in Babelsberg, 1960er Jahre.

Das Haupthaus des Campus in Griebnitzsee empfiehlt sich immer wieder mal als Filmkulisse. Das Herzstück des Geländes ist das älteste und sicher auch eindrucksvollste Gebäude am Ort. Seit 1896 war das Areal im Besitz des Deutschen Roten Kreuzes. Zwischen 1939 und 1943 entstand dann der Monumentalbau, der noch in den letzten Kriegsjahren als Präsidialgebäude des DRK diente. Einige Jahre nach dem Ende des Krieges zog die Deutsche Verwaltungsakademie nach Babelsberg und blieb (später als Akademie für Staats- und Rechtswissenschaft) bis 1989. Das präsidiale Äußere und die nationalsozialistische Geschichte des Hauses spielten tatsächlich in den 1980er Jahren noch eine (Haupt-)Rolle: bei den Dreharbeiten für den Film „Mephisto" in der Regie von István Szabó.

The main building on Griebnitzsee campus provides an almost cinematic front. The heart of the premises is the oldest and most impressive building on the spot. The whole area was in possession of the German Red Cross since 1896. The monumental building was erected between 1939 and 1943 and was used as headquarters in the last years of World War II. A few years after the war the German Administration Academy moved to Babelsberg and stayed (later as Academy of Political Sciences and Jurisprudence) until 1989. The presidential exterior and the national socialist history of the building actually played a (leading) role in the 1980s again: during the shooting of the film "Mephisto" directed by István Szabó.

Hauptgebäude des Campus Griebnitzsee, 2011.

Wachturm an der innerdeutschen Grenze in Potsdam-Babelsberg, 1989.

Durch seine Lage zwischen zwei nach West-Berlin führenden Bahnstrecken sowie seine direkte Nachbarschaft zur Berliner Enklave Steinstücken war das Gelände des heutigen Campus Griebnitzsee seit 1945 Grenzland. Unübersehbar wurde dies mit dem Bau der Berliner Mauer 1961: Sie umfasste fast zwei Drittel des gesamten Areals, das wie eine Pfeilspitze ins Gebiet des „Klassenfeinds" zu ragen schien. Teilweise verlief die Mauer nur wenige Meter vor den Fenstern der Gebäude entlang und durchschnitt Grundstücke und Wege gleichermaßen, von Wachtürmen gesäumt. Mittlerweile sind die Straßen wieder verbunden und der einst öde Sandstreifen Standort der universitären Neubauten.

Due to its location between two railway tracks leading to West-Berlin as well as its direct neighbourhood to the enclave "Steinstücken" the area of today's Griebnitzsee campus had been borderland since 1945. This became highly visible when the Berlin Wall was built in 1961: it encompassed almost two thirds of the whole site, which seemed to protrude like an arrowhead into the "class enemy's" territory. At some points the Wall ran only a few meters in front of the buildings und cut through properties and paths likewise, lined by watchtowers. Today the streets are reconnected and the once deserted sand strip is now the site of the university's new buildings.

An der Stadtgrenze zwischen Potsdam und Berlin, 2011.

„Todesstreifen" rund um das Gelände der Akademie für Staats- und Rechtswissenschaft, 1989.

Südlich des Hauptgebäudes verlief bis 1989 die Berliner Mauer, ringsum erstreckte sich der kahle Sandstreifen der verbotenen Zone. Gleich nach der Öffnung der Grenze begannen die „Mauerspechte" damit, den Grenzwall zu durchlöchern, bald ganz abzutragen. Dort, wo einst Grenztruppen patrouillierten, steht heute ein Studentendorf. Es ist eines von vielen Wohnheimen, die das Studentenwerk in der Stadt betreibt. 543 Zimmer, verteilt auf neun Häuser gibt es hier. Vor den Fenstern der Studenten verläuft nach wie vor eine Grenze, doch heute ist es nur noch die Stadtgrenze von Potsdam nach Berlin.

The Berlin Wall ran south of the main building until 1989 and all around spread the bare sand strip of the forbidden zone. Soon after the fall of the Wall the so called "wallpeckers", people who hacked pieces out of the Wall as souvenirs, started to perforate the ramparts, and soon cleared it away completely. Where there were once border patrols there is a student village today. It is one of many residential halls run by the "Studentenwerk", the student services office. In the nine houses on campus Griebnitzsee there are 543 rooms altogether. Outside of the students rooms there is still a border, but today it's only the city limit between Potsdam and Berlin.

Studentendorf in Griebnitzsee, 2007.

Gebäude aus der Zeit des DRK, Sitz der Wirtschafts- und Sozialwissenschaftlichen Fakultät, 1995.

Nachdem die Universität Potsdam 1991 den Campus in Griebnitzsee übernommen hatte, zog die Wirtschafts- und Sozialwissenschaftliche Fakultät hierher. Vor allem die beiden im Heimatstil gestalteten Häuser wurden alsbald zu ihrem Markenzeichen. Doch seit der Fertigstellung des neuen Hörsaalgebäudes 2007 nutzen vor allem ihre Studierenden die zusätzlichen Räume. Innen Sichtbeton und außen rot-violette Ringofenziegel ergänzen das vorhandene „vielgesichtige" historische Ensemble behutsam und doch erkennbar.

Soon after the university took over the premises in Griebnitzsee in 1991, the Faculty of Economics and Social Sciences moved there. Especially the two buildings in the traditional local style became the faculty's trademark. But since the new lecture building was finished in 2007 the students primarily use the additional rooms. Raw concrete on the inside and reddish-purple bricks on the outside complement the existing multi-faceted historic ensemble gently but visibly.

Institutsgebäude auf dem Campus Griebnitzsee mit dem Hörsaalneubau (links), 2011.

Garagen auf dem Gelände der Akademie für Staats- und Rechtswissenschaft, 1980er Jahre.

Während die Universität Potsdam 2011 ihr 20-jähriges Jubiläum feiert, ist das Hasso-Plattner-Institut gerade einmal zwölf Jahre alt – und doch schon äußerst erfolgreich. Das nach seinem Stifter, einem der Firmengründer von SAP, benannte An-Institut nahm 1999 im Eiltempo seinen Studienbetrieb auf. 2001 konnten die neu errichteten Institutsgebäude in Griebnitzsee bezogen werden. Im Juli 2010 kam ein Erweiterungsbau hinzu. Dazwischen liegt die Geschichte eines Erfolges: Rund 460 Bachelor- und 190 Masterabsolventen haben bis 2009 am HPI ihr Studium im IT-Systems Engineering abgeschlossen. Seit 2004 belegt das Institut Spitzenränge bei Evaluationen und es wurde bereits dreimal als „ausgewählter Ort" im „Land der Ideen" ausgezeichnet.

While the University of Potsdam is celebrating its 20th anniversary in 2011, the Hasso-Plattner-Institute is only 12 years old – but already very successful. The institute, which was named after its benefactor, one of the co-founders of SAP, has a cooperation agreement with the university and commenced its academic work in a rush in 1999. In 2001 they moved into the newly build premises in Griebnitzsee. In July 2010 an additional building was opened. In-between lies a story of success: about 460 bachelor and 190 master graduates have completed their IT-Systems Engineering studies at the HPI until 2009, and since 2004 the institute reached highest ranks in various evaluations and was three times nominated "Selected Location" in the campaign "Germany – Land of Ideas".

Hasso-Plattner-Institut, 2011.

Umbau der früheren DRK-Baracke zum Bibliotheksgebäude, 2000.

Das Haus der Bibliothek in Griebnitzsee war schon immer ein Lagerort. Allerdings gab es in der Baracke zur Zeit ihrer Nutzung durch das Deutsche Rote Kreuz bis 1945 nur Kleidung, danach andere Güter und Waren. Erst die Universität Potsdam brachte Bücher hier unter. Durch eine vollständige Sanierung entstand im Jahr 2000 eine moderne, funktionale Bibliothek. Diese hat nicht nur mit 250 000 Büchern die Bestände von Rechts-, Wirtschafts- und Sozialwissenschaften aufgenommen, sondern ist – v.a. dank der über den Buchregalen liegenden Empore – ein Schmuckstück geworden.

The library building in Griebnitzsee has always been a storage location. Until 1945 the barrack was used by the German Red Cross for the storage of clothes, later also for other goods. It was the University of Potsdam that turned it into a 'storage location' for books. During a complete reconstruction in 2000 the barrack was turned into a modern, functional library. The building holds 250,000 books, the stock of the jurisprudence, economic and social studies. Thanks to the gallery above the shelves it also became a real architectural gem.

Bibliothek auf dem Campus Griebnitzsee, 2011.

Studenten im Lesesaal der Pädagogischen Hochschule „Karl Liebknecht", 1974.

Hörsaal, Labor, Feldarbeit oder Sporthalle – studieren kann vieles bedeuten. Aber egal, welches Fach man belegt, am Selbststudium ist nach wie vor kein Vorbeikommen. Allerdings haben sich die Möglichkeiten des Lernens vervielfacht. Einsame Lektüre im stillen Kämmerlein ist schon lange nicht mehr der alleinige Weg zum Erfolg. Digitale Publikationen, e-Learning, Lerngruppen uvm. verändern die Studienkultur nachhaltig. Auf diesen Wandel hat sich die Universität Potsdam eingestellt, nicht zuletzt bei der Ausstattung ihrer drei neuen Bereichsbibliotheken. Und wer will, kann sich auch weiterhin einfach aus dem Bestand der rund 1,3 Millionen Bücher bedienen.

Lecture hall, laboratory, field work or gymnasium – studying can mean a lot of things. But no matter which subject one chooses, no one can get past the self-study. But certainly the possibilities of mediation have multiplied. Secluded reading in small chambers is no longer the exclusive way to success. Digital publications, e-learning, study groups and a lot more have changed the way of studying effectively. The University of Potsdam has adjusted to this change, not least in the facilities of its three libraries. But whoever feels like it can still make use of the stock of 1.3 million books.

Studenten in der Babelsberger Bibliothek, 2011.

Chemie-Vorlesung an der Pädagogischen Hochschule „Karl Liebknecht", 1970er Jahre.

Es gibt Schüler, die in der Schule immer auf Chemie warten, weil sie der Bunsenbrenner, schmelzendes Plastik und blubbernde Flüssigkeiten in großen Kolben begeistern. Freilich: Dahinter steht das hart erarbeitete Wissen von den Elementen. Groß ist die Freude, wenn die neuen Studenten feststellen, dass eine Vorlesung an der Uni denselben Forschergeist vermittelt, der sie zum Studium des einen oder anderen Fachs gebracht hat – und der mitunter ebenso farbenfroh, laut oder geruchsintensiv daherkommt. Dabei integrieren sich Computertechnologie und der obligatorische Kittel gleichermaßen perfekt in das Königreich der Elemente.

There are pupils who cannot wait for their chemistry classes in school because they get all excited about Bunsen burners, melting plastic and bubbling fluids in big flasks. Of course, there is hard-earned knowledge of the elements behind that. The new students are overwhelmed when they realize that the lectures at the university include the same spirit of research which brought them to study one or the other subject - a spirit of research that can be quite colourful, loud or smelly. At the same time new computer technologies and the obligatory white lab coat blend in perfectly with the realm of the elements.

Chemie-Vorlesung, 2009.

Chor der Pädagogischen Hochschule, 1960er Jahre.

Wo musiziert wird, fallen Töne. Und an der Potsdamer Uni, wo – schon seit den Zeiten der Pädagogischen Hochschule – nicht nur Musikwissenschaftler, sondern auch die entsprechenden Pädagogen ausgebildet werden, sind es gleich ein paar mehr. Seit 1996 gibt es mit „Campus Cantabile" einen 50-köpfigen Chor, der auch schon mal Bachs Weihnachtsoratorium aufführt. Bereits 1997 kam ein Orchester – „Sinfonietta Potsdam" – hinzu, das mittlerweile im Potsdamer Nikolaisaal gern gehörter Gast ist. Und spätestens seit der Entstehung des studentischen Chores „Uni-Sono" und der Band „Schwungkollegium" klingen auch andere Töne an.

Wherever there is music there are notes. And at the University of Potsdam, where – even in the times of the teacher training college – not only musicologists are trained but also the corresponding teachers, there are even a bit more. Since 1996 there is "Campus Cantabile", a choir of 50 people that among other pieces performs Bach's Christmas Oratorio. Then in 1997 an orchestra – "Sinfonietta Potsdam" – was founded, which is a well-liked guest in Potsdam's concert hall Nikolaisaal. And since the establishment of the student choir "Uni-Sono" and the band "Schwungkollegium" very different tones can be heard.

Konzert des Orchesters „Sinfonietta Potsdam" und des Chors „Campus Cantabile" der Universität im Nikolaisaal, 2006.

Studentin mit Kindern, 1974.

Erst Schule und Studium, dann Kinder? Wer eine Familie möchte, plant das meist so. Andere, die nicht planen oder nicht warten wollen, versuchen das eine mit dem anderen in Einklang zu bringen. Gerade für viele Lehramtsstudenten, die in der DDR an der Pädagogischen Hochschule studierten, gehörten Kinder selbstverständlich zum Studium dazu. Dafür, dass das auch heute möglich ist – immerhin haben von den 20 000 Studierenden an der Universität Potsdam rund 1400 bereits Kinder –, engagiert sich das Büro für Chancengleichheit. So gibt es an allen drei Standorten Räume für Eltern und Kinder, eine eigene Betriebskita auf dem Campus Am Neuen Palais und ein aktives Elternnetzwerk.

First school and university, then children? Whoever wants a family thinks in that order. Others who did not plan or could not wait try to harmonise one with the other. For those who studied for a teaching degree at the teacher training college in the GDR, children were a normal part of their student's life. In order to make that possible today – after all, 1,400 of the 20,000 students at the university already have children – the office for equal opportunities gets involved. There are rooms for parents and their children at all three campuses, an in-house daycare center at the campus Am Neuen Palais and an active parent network.

Studentin mit Kind, 2007.

Konzert bei den FDJ-Studententagen an der Pädagogischen Hochschule „Karl Liebknecht", 1984.

Studentische Kultur hat einen unschlagbaren Vorteil: Sie braucht fast nichts, um sich selbst auf die Beine oder Bühne zu stellen. Eine Gitarre, eine Stimme und einer, der zuhört, machen ein Konzert. Natürlich ist das kein Grund, nicht auch mal eine Bühne aus dem Nichts zu zaubern und alles, was musiziert, draufzustellen. Einzige Bedingung: Es sollte möglichst mitten auf dem Campus geschehen. So oder ähnlich stellen die Studenten jedes Jahr an der Potsdamer Universität ein Sommerfest auf die Beine, das nicht zuletzt von der Vielfalt der Musiker lebt, die dafür zusammenkommen.

Student culture has one particular advantage: it does not take a lot to get up and going. A guitar, a voice and someone who listens already make a concert. Of course there is no reason not to conjure a stage from scratch and put anything on it that makes music. Under one condition: it should happen right on campus. Every year students of the University of Potsdam organise a summer festival in a similar fashion, that - if nothing else - lives from diverse musicians that come together for that purpose.

Gastkonzert der schwedischen Band „Renhornen“, 2011.

Essenausgabe in der Oberen Mensa an der Pädagogischen Hochschule „Karl Liebknecht", 1974.

Essen für 20 000 Studenten – einkaufen, kochen, verteilen und: abwaschen? Es mag Zeiten gegeben haben, wo die Essenausgabe einer Mensa in Potsdam Ähnlichkeiten mit einer Feldküche der Armee hatte und alle hielten das für eine logistische Meisterleistung. Inzwischen sind die Mensen zu universitären Umschlagplätzen mit Hightech-Ausstattung geworden, die mitunter Transit-Bahnhöfen gleichen: Sitzecken, Anzeigetafeln, Ausgabeschalter und Kassen mit Chipkartenlesern. Der Blick zurück macht zwar nicht satt, aber vielleicht ein bisschen geduldiger, wenn man einmal kurz in der Schlange steht.

Meals for 20,000 students – shopping for ingredients, cooking, giving out the meals and cleaning the dishes? There may have been times when the food counter of the cafeteria in Potsdam had similarities with a field kitchen of the army and everyone thought of it as a logistic master piece. Meanwhile, the cafeterias have become academic hubs with high-tech equipment which sometimes appear like airport gates: sitting areas, display panels, issuing counters and cashiers with smartcard readers. Looking back on that does not fill one's stomach but it might make one more patient when standing in line for a short while.

Mensa auf dem Campus Golm, 2011.

Akademie-Standort im Park Babelsberg, 1988.

„Studieren im Park“ konnte man bis vor Kurzem nicht nur auf dem Campus Am Neuen Palais, sondern auch im Park Babelsberg. Die von der Akademie für Staats- und Rechtswissenschaft übernommenen Gebäude wurden lange von den Wirtschafts- und Sozialwissenschaftlern genutzt. Inzwischen ist der Standort weitgehend aufgegeben und das Areal wieder in die einzigartige Landschaft des Parks integriert. Geblieben ist das Studentenwohnheim, dessen Bewohner nun ungestört im Grünen wohnen. Wer heute über den Hügel, an dem die Mensa stand, in Richtung des Babelsberger Schlosses geht, blickt wieder direkt auf die Havel – und auf das Zeichen des politischen Wandels von 1989/90 schlechthin: die Glienicker Brücke.

Until recently one could not only "study in the park" at Am Neuen Palais campus but also at Park Babelsberg campus. The buildings taken over from the Academy of Political Science and Jurisprudence were used by the Faculty of Economics and Social Sciences for a long time. In the meantime the facilities have been abandoned more or less and the site has been almost reintegrated into the unique landscape of the park. The residential hall has remained and its residents now live close to nature. Walking across the hill, where the cafeteria once was, towards Babelsberg Castle one looks directly to the river "Havel" – and the symbol for political change in 1989/90 par excellence: the Glienicke Bridge.

Blick auf die Glienicker Brücke vom Park Babelsberg, 2009.